Westward to
Promontory

It was a grand Anvil Chorus that
those pounding sledges were playing
across the plains and mountains,
in triple time: three strokes to
the spike; ten spikes to the rail;
400 rails to the mile; 425 miles
in 1868 on the road to Promontory
and the completion of
the great work of the age...

Westward to Promontory

Building the Union Pacific across the plains and mountains

A PICTORIAL DOCUMENTARY

with text by

BARRY B. COMBS

Published by
CROWN PUBLISHERS, INC.
with the cooperation of
THE OAKLAND MUSEUM and UNION PACIFIC CORPORATION

Published in cooperation with The Oakland Museum and
Union Pacific Corporation by Crown Publishers, Inc., 225 Park
Avenue South, New York, New York 10003

CROWN is a trademark of Crown Publishers, Inc.

Manufactured in Italy

Library of Congress Cataloging-in-Publication Data

Russell, Andrew J.
    Westward to Promontory.

    "The Andrew J. Russell negatives . . . form part of the
photographic archives of the Oakland Museum"—
    "Published in cooperation with the Oakland Museum and
Union Pacific Corporation"—T.p. verso.
    1. Union Pacific Railroad.   I. Combs, Barry.
II. Oakland Museum.   III. Union Pacific Corporation.
IV. Title.
TF25.U5R88   1986   625.1'0978   86-2318

ISBN 0-517-56223-5

ISBN 0-517-56224-3 (pbk.)

10   9   8   7   6   5   4   3   2   1

First Revised Edition

FOREWORD

Early in 1969, The Oakland Museum acquired a remarkable historic record—a large collection of collodion glass-plate negatives depicting in intimate detail the building of the transcontinental railroad during the years 1868–69. These fragile and unique documents, consisting of some two hundred 10 × 13-inch wet-plate negatives and more than four hundred stereoscopic negatives, were discovered by William D. Pattison, Professor of Geography at the University of Chicago, in the archives of the American Geographical Society in New York after being lost for nearly a century. The records of the Society attributed the photographs to Stephen J. Sedgwick, a popular nineteenth-century lecturer whose "illuminated lectures" on the world's religions, natural history, and the Pacific Railroad afforded him considerable prominence. But it remained for Professor Pattison to determine the true identity of the master photographer who traveled the plains and mountains with his large-format camera and bulky materials to record the joining of East and West by a transcontinental railroad. Pattison's study of the inscriptions

Andrew J. Russell
Tintype courtesy of Elizabeth Gamble Johnson, great granddaughter of Andrew J. Russell

5

scratched by the photographer in the emulsion of the plates led him to the discovery that they were the work of Andrew J. Russell, former official photographer to the United States Military Railroad during the Civil War.

In 1868, at the age of thirty-eight, Russell had embarked on an expedition to document the construction of the Union Pacific portion of the transcontinental railroad. At times proclaimed the official photographer for Union Pacific Railroad, Russell had the complete cooperation of the railroad as he traveled from railheads to construction camps. Three separate trips were made along the line—one in 1868 and two in 1869.

Russell used an outdoor camera of his own design, which he described in *Anthony's Photographic Bulletin* in 1870: "I cannot but think that outdoor photographers in general will be thankful for any improvement in apparatus, especially in making the work of carrying lighter, and at the same time economizing room and giving durability. The box I present to your readers is both compact, durable, light and convenient, and is far from being complicated in its construction. . . ." Improvement indeed! This cumbersome box, its giant lens, the boxes of heavy—and fragile—glass plates for exposing negatives, and the array of chemicals posed a challenge of alchemy and art for photographer Russell. The laborious, slow "wet-plate" process of the time required that each glass-plate negative be prepared just before use—its collodion emulsion had to remain damp during exposure and processing or the negative would lose its sensitivity. In conditions from blazing heat to bitter cold, Russell had to coat each plate with collodion, and then sensitize, expose, develop, and fix it wherever he chanced upon a scene he wanted to picture. He left his most telling revelation until last: a caption describing the scene, scratched in his own hand in the emulsion. Russell also photographed with a stereoscopic-view camera, producing a double-image negative. When printed and viewed through a stereo viewer—the television set of Victorian parlors—a single three-dimensional image emerged. The more than four hundred stereo negatives taken by the artist were published by Russell himself when he returned to his New York City studio in 1870, and again later by promoter and entrepreneur Sedgwick, who touted the views as his own.

Russell was raised in Nunda, a small frontier town in western New York. He began as a local painter with interests in both landscape and portraiture, and eventually established a studio in New York City in 1859. The outbreak of the Civil War riveted Russell's attention and emotions. From published woodcut images of the war, Russell painted a large, revolving twenty-four section diorama entitled "Panorama of the War for the Union," which the *Nunda News* described as exhibiting "more than 400,000 persons, 10,000 horses and carriages, many of which appear life size . . ."—a patriotic zeal of epic proportions. In 1862, Russell enlisted as Captain in the 141st Regiment, New York Infantry. In 1863, he was detached to Alexandria, Virginia, as official photographer to the United States Military Railroad. There, provided with a camera by the government, Russell joined General Herman Haupt, head of the United States Military Railroad Construction Corps, as "photographer artist." At Alexandria, Fredericksburg, City Point, and Richmond, the might of America's industrial age and the mass destruction of the conflict were captured by Russell in striking images that were later misattributed to Mathew Brady.

It was the lure of the building of the transcontinental railroad, "The Great Work of the Age," that drew Russell west along with other veterans of both the Union and the Confederacy, some still wearing the remnants of their Civil War uniforms (p. 63). From Omaha to Promontory Summit, Utah, Russell traversed "The Great American Desert" with the Union Pacific Railroad construction crews, capturing the spirit of a still young nation on the move in a vast landscape inhabited by the unstoppable iron horse and its keepers. Here, Russell achieves mastery of his discipline, the complete "photographer artist." For the first time, man, nature, and machine are inextricably linked in a new photographic vision of the American landscape, one in which the machine and its trappings have assumed an equal place with the wonders of nature.

Russell's most famous photograph, "East and West Shaking Hands at Laying of Last Rail," captures the self-congratulatory final moment as men and machines link up at Promontory Summit to join a continent and underscore the fulfillment of America's Manifest Destiny. The implications of this event were not lost on Russell, for he wrote soon after: "The great railroad problem of the age is now solved. The continental iron band now permanently unites the distant portions of the Republic and opens up to commerce, navigation, and enterprise the vast unpeopled plains and lofty mountain ranges that divide the East from the West." Andrew J. Russell's work was finished, but the power of his images lives on in the pages that follow. What Russell compiled was a visual and historical record of this great enterprise, which stands as one of the most important treasures of American photography—indeed, of American history.

The Andrew J. Russell negatives from which this book was created now form part of the photographic archives of The Oakland Museum, a regional museum devoted to the history, art, and natural sciences of California and the West. These photographic negatives are primary historical documents. The importance of this collection to the Museum is reflected in the planned debut of a major traveling exhibition in 1987 (the 125th anniversary of the Pacific Railroad Act) in conjunction with the International Center of Photography, and further publications on the distinguished work of Andrew J. Russell. The Oakland Museum is honored to join with Union Pacific and Crown Publishers to present this revised edition of *Westward to Promontory*.

L. Thomas Frye
Chief Curator of History
The Oakland Museum
June, 1986

Across the Continent: "Westward the Course of Empire Takes Its Way"—this lithograph of the 1850's, reeking with symbolism, typified the continental urge that led to the completion of the great American railroad.

WESTWARD . . .

For generations, the edge of the American frontier had moved inexorably westward—over the Appalachians, into the valley of the Ohio, through the Cumberland Gap, into the bluegrass of Kentucky, and on until it reached the rich valley of the Mississippi. And there, for a time, it stopped, banked up against the edge of the North American interior, a high, semi-arid, treeless plain slowly rising to meet a series of seemingly impassable mountain ranges. It was a country outside a frontier experience formed in the lakes, rivers, woods, and rich bottomlands of the eastern third of the continent.

The barrier was emotional as well as physical. In 1820, Major Stephen Harriman Long led an expedition of scientists into the trans-Mississippi wilderness and put on it a name that would last for another forty years: "The Great American Desert." It was, he said, "almost wholly unfit for cultivation, and of course uninhabitable by a people depending upon agriculture for their subsistence," a resoundingly inaccurate description that nevertheless discouraged settlement. So the frontier jumped over the American interior to California, Oregon, and Washington, until the continental population was divided by a sparsely settled midsection nearly two thousand miles across.

The dream of linking these two sections by a railroad began early, and was tied to another grand American dream: tapping the commerce of Asia via a land route across the continent. This had been one of the goals of the Lewis and Clark expedition of 1803, and it remained a shining hope in the minds of eastern entrepreneurs, who would have dearly welcomed a shortcut to the markets of Asia. One of these was a New York merchant named Asa Whitney, who in 1844 made a proposition to Congress that was, to say the least, unusual. He proposed that Congress sell him a strip of land—at sixteen cents an acre—from Wisconsin to the Pacific Ocean. He told the lawmakers he wanted his land sixty miles wide and he would use it to build them a railroad. Construction would be financed by selling off the land a little bit at a time. First, said Whitney, he would build a few miles of railroad, making the land around it valuable, then sell off that land and with the money build more railroad, repeating the process from Milwaukee to the mouth of the Columbia River on the Pacific Ocean. In twenty-five years, he prophesied, the nation would have a railroad through which the treasure of the Orient would flow.

Whitney was a man with an idea right for his time. In the mid-1840's his concept of a Pacific Railroad meshed perfectly with an idea that was already sweeping the country—Manifest Destiny. It was our manifest destiny, said continentalists, "to overspread and to possess the whole of the continent which Providence has given us for the development of the great experiment of liberty and federated self-government. . . ."

What better way to realize our destiny than with a great railroad to the sea? It was a magical idea. Whitney had opened the gates and the flood-waters of political oratory poured forth. Unfortunately, not everyone agreed with his choice for a starting point. A young Congressman from Illinois had a better idea. Build the railroad, by all means, said Stephen A. Douglas, but let it begin in Chicago, not Milwaukee. No, said the editor of the Police Gazette, Independence, Missouri, is the rightful place from which to begin. John C. Calhoun, spokesman for the South, led a Memphis convention to champion that city. Before long, sectional lines for the fight to come had been drawn.

No one really believed that more than one transcontinental railroad would ever be built. Therefore the city or section from which it led would have an overwhelming commercial advantage. The chosen city would "rival Carthage in her pride of power—the great commercial emporium of the Mississippi Valley, into whose commission houses would pour the commerce of the world."

Almost without exception, early promoters of the railroad based their argument on the promise of trade with Asia. Years later, Union Pacific Railroad president Sidney Dillon recalled, "The real objective point continued to be China and Japan and the Asiatic trade." It was ironic that just six months after the driving of the last spike at Promontory, the first ship sailed through the Suez Canal and put an end to this hope.

Other arguments for the railroad bore better fruit. By 1850 Manifest Destiny and the politics of James K. Polk had added enough new real estate to eventually carve out nine new states, including California, Oregon, and Texas. In 1849, during the onslaught of the gold rush, ninety thousand people arrived in California. Other thousands were filling Oregon's rich valleys with farms. To reach their promised land, these Pacific Coast pioneers had two choices—by sea or wagon trail. The sea route was expensive and dangerous, involving either a lengthy voyage around Cape Horn or portage across the fever-infested Isthmus of Panama. By land, the disadvantages were almost as great: the danger of Indian attack, long waterless stretches, enormous physical exertion, and torturous slowness. (One hundred days from the Missouri River to California was good time.)

But still they came, and in increasing numbers. Once there, the settlers' bonds with the East—the 'States' as they called it—were tenuous ones at best: memory, citizenship, and a trickle of mail that took weeks and sometimes months for delivery.

Champions of the Pacific Railroad seized on California's isolation and used it as an argument more acceptable to Congress than those of commerce. A railroad would bind the two parts of the nation together, greatly multiplying trade and creating political unity. What if a foreign power (Great Britain was the usual scapegoat) were to attack our new settlements? How could they be defended?

Other arguments concerned themselves with settling the plains. No less than three hundred thousand immigrants arrived in the nation every year between 1845 and 1855. Many of the newcomers were farmers, and pressure increased to open the plains to settlement. But settlement could not come to the plains without some form of transportation faster and more economical than ox-drawn freight wagons. And settlement could not take place before the original inhabitants, the Indians, were subdued. Both of these disadvantages could be solved by the building of a transcontinental railroad—to carry the settlers' produce out and the army in.

So many arguments for building a railroad were advanced that it seemed the only problem to be solved was that of just where the line would be. Legislation was advanced and defeated repeatedly. The sectional lines that had been drawn earlier hardened. Finally, in 1853, when it was obvious that no section could gain the advantage over another, Congress de-

A view of the "Great American Desert" in 1822, when it still was a region penetrated only by laboring pack trains and known intimately only to the peripatetic fur trapper and the Indian. In a little more than a generation, the shining rails of empire would strike across the vast plains and mountains to Promontory.

cided to step aside and let Mother Nature decide. Several alternate routes would be surveyed, and the railroad would follow the one found most economical and practical.

Thus began the most exhaustive investigation of the American West that had been made to that time. The Department of War put four main parties into the field. Botanists, geologists, artists, naturalists, zoologists, engineers, and cartographers accompanied them. Beginning in 1853, with a preliminary report in 1855, survey parties finally presented their findings in a set of eleven handsome quarto volumes in 1857. Unfortunately, the result of this mass of information was only to further confuse the issue. It appeared there were **several** practicable routes for a Pacific Railroad. Secretary of War Jefferson Davis further muddied the water by throwing his support to the southernmost route when he presented the reports to Congress. This route, the future president of the Confederacy pointed out, would be the least expensive. Perhaps so, but no northern congressman hopeful of re-election would support it.

Thus, by 1860, the issue remained almost where it had begun—stranded on the question of sectionalism, a question that was becoming more intense as the nation drifted toward civil war.

Still the need for a Pacific Railroad persisted. By 1860, California's population had increased to three hundred thousand. The steady rain of petitions for the railroad continued to fall on a Congress unable to act. At the same time the tide of European immigration poured more and more people into the cities of the East and increased their land hunger. It was a dilemma which would not be resolved short of civil war.

On April 12, 1861, Fort Sumter was fired on. Three weeks later eleven southern states had seceded and the nation was plunged into conflict. Congress was left bereft of its southern members and all opposition to a northern route vanished. Ironically, it had required the dissolution of the Union to clear the way for the project the whole nation had supported only a few years earlier.

That the Pacific Railroad would require federal support had long been accepted by even the most dedicated supporters of free enterprise. The undertaking would absorb huge amounts of capital with no promise of return until it was finished, and this, many thought, would be at least ten years. Some form of cooperation between private capital and government aid had been the goal of every booster of the road since Asa Whitney made his original proposition.

Such a combination formed the basis of the bill passed by both houses of Congress in May and June of 1862 and signed into law by Abraham Lincoln on July 1. Called the Pacific Railroad Act, it sought to entice private investment by endowing the railroad corporation with a grant of government lands and a loan of government bonds.

The act chartered a corporation to be known as Union Pacific Railroad Company, to which this aid would be given. At the first meeting of the new company in October, 1863, thirty directors were chosen, among them General John A. Dix as president and Thomas C. Durant as vice-president. Since Dix never really assumed the duties and responsibilities of the office, Durant soon worked his way into the position of being the Union Pacific's chief promoter and financial engineer. The act also bestowed federal beneficence on the Central Pacific Railroad Company, an enterprise chartered under California law a year earlier. C.P. was to build east to the state line. U.P. would build west from the Missouri River across the Nebraska plains, over the Rockies, and through the Great Salt Lake Basin until it met the rails of the California company.

Just exactly where on the Missouri River the rails were to start Congress was not about to specify. Central route or no, there was still entirely too much rivalry between river towns in Missouri, Kansas, Iowa, and Nebraska. That job Congress left to the President, who eventually chose the point where Council Bluffs and Omaha faced each other across the Missouri.

The grant of land was to be measured in miles of road built. For each mile, the railroad would receive ten sections (six hundred forty acres each) of the public domain, but only the alternate sections ten miles back from each side of the track. Uncle Sam held on to the intervening sections and promptly doubled their price in the confidence that their proximity to the railroad would ensure a quick sale. Thus in Nebraska, for instance, the federal government granted lands that had remained unsold on the market for eight years and ensured that they would recover their paper loss from the land grant as soon as the railroad was built.

Part two of the federal aid package consisted of the loan of government bonds. Again on a mileage basis, the bonds were parceled out at the rate of $16,000 per mile of level ground, $32,000 per mile for foothills, and $48,000 per mile for mountainous terrain. They were to be repaid in thirty years at six per cent interest.

No one pretended that federal aid alone would be enough to build a railroad. It was designed only to act as a lure to attract enough private capital to do the job. In this it failed dismally. When the stock of the great national enterprise hit the market in October, 1862, investors stayed away

Muscle, sweat, and iron: With driving energy, track gangs like these laid down four hundred twenty-five miles of rail in 1868.

When the rails reached the 100th meridian, two hundred forty-seven miles west of Omaha, U. P. Vice-President Thomas C. Durant threw a three-day party. Above, a special excursion train filled with journalists, tycoons, and royalty reaches the end of track. Photograph by John Carbutt.

in droves. The first offering sold only thirty-one shares—hardly enough to build a railroad to the sea. The Pacific Railroad Act would have to be amended, the government's share increased, the lure sweetened. Two years later, the land grant was doubled and the bond loan was altered from a first to a second mortgage.

In the meantime actual work got under way. On the cold wintery morning of December 2, 1863, most of the citizens of the frontier villages of Omaha and Council Bluffs gathered on the Missouri River mud flats, listened to suitable speeches by the governor of Nebraska and the mayors of the two towns, and then applauded the official ground breaking for the Union Pacific Railroad. It was an auspicious start, and grading got under way immediately. Eighteen months later the first rail was still unlaid.

Compounding the money problems of the infant railroad was that of supply. When ground was broken the nearest railroad was still more than one hundred miles away and wouldn't reach Council Bluffs for four more years. The treacherous currents of the Missouri River provided Omaha's chief source of transportation upriver from St. Joseph, Missouri. Sandbanks in the Missouri were littered with the wrecks of river boats. Rails had to be brought in from the East. Even crossties were a problem, since hardwood was scarce along the river and didn't exist out on the plains. To add to all this, the Civil War had skyrocketed the price of materials and monopolized available venture capital.

After the surrender at Appomattox, Union Pacific's fortunes changed radically for the better. Ready workers, many of them fresh from the Union and Confederate armies, flocked to Omaha in search of adventure and the high pay the railroad was offering. Iron for rails, spikes, and locomotives became available, as did the necessary investment capital with which to buy them.

One of the greatest postwar boons to the railroad was the release from military service of a young major general with a strong background in civil engineering and railroad building. His name was Grenville M. Dodge, and he came to Omaha in 1865 to take over as Union Pacific's chief engineer, hired by Thomas C. Durant. Durant and Dodge made a curious pair. Durant was everything the serious engineer was not. A flashy dresser, sharp-tempered, completely knowledgeable in the shifting money market of the immediate postwar years, Durant provided the funds and the political favors to make the building of the road possible. Dodge supplied the drive, the organizational ability and technical skill that got the job done in the face of overwhelming physical problems. By the end of 1865 he had pushed the rails forty miles into Nebraska Territory.

Once past the Omaha foothills, the rails followed the Platte River Valley westward for nearly four hundred miles. It was a route Dodge had long known. As a young surveyor for the Rock Island Railroad in 1853 (then preparing to build in Iowa), Dodge had inspected the point where the Platte empties into the Missouri just below Omaha. He stood then on a high hill and looked west up the broad Platte Valley. It was, it seemed to him, an ideal route for a railroad to the West: "The Lord had so constructed the country that any engineer who failed to take advantage of the great open road . . . would not have been fit to belong to the profession." Dodge took advantage of it. In 1866 construction speed picked up and two hundred fifty more miles were added, bringing end-of-track to a point near present-day North Platte, Nebraska.

Thomas C. Durant was not a man to miss the natural opportunity for publicity—especially if it would help market the railroad's securities. In the fall of 1866, when the rails reached the 100th meridian of longitude, Durant decided to celebrate. It mattered not that this geographical point lay many miles from the nearest settlement—two hundred forty-seven miles west of Omaha and civilization (whether Omaha in 1866 truly represented civilization was a point many Easterners seriously questioned). Durant would have his party on the spot. His invitation list read like a "Who's Who" of American and European politics and business, including high-ranking politicians, financiers, journalists, a marquis, and an earl. The several hundred guests came by rail to St. Joseph, Missouri, the closest railhead to Omaha, then boarded river boats for the trip upstream. At Omaha they were entertained royally with a banquet and ball, and bustled on board a sumptuous excursion train, which included four out of the five first-class passenger cars the infant railroad owned.

They spent three days out on the prairie, and tented out each night in a luxurious version of western camp life. Durant had arranged several diversions for his guests. The first night, they thrilled to a staged Indian war dance—then thrilled even more when the hired Indians staged a mock raid on their camp later that same night.

The next day they watched a sham Indian battle—also prearranged by Durant—and posed for photographs at the 100th meridian in the midst of a seemingly endless prairie. That night the excursionists were entertained by vaudeville acts and a band concert, and the next day went on to the actual end-of-track to watch the Irish workmen laying the rails that would span the continent.

Almost as an afterthought, Durant saved his most spectacular act for their last night out. He arranged to have the prairie set on fire. His guests

In 1866, Missouri steamboats unloaded Durant's excursionists at Omaha for the train ride to the end of the line. Photograph by John Carbutt.

The construction of the transcontinental line was "the great work of the age," and with its completion came the great age of American railroading—Silver Palace Sleeping Coaches, superb cuisine, and only six days and twenty hours from San Francisco to New York.

watched in exhausted awe from the safety of their cars as a twenty-mile stretch of dry prairie grass sent flames leaping into the Nebraska night.

Dodge, the serious engineer, privately wondered if all this was the proper way to run a railroad. For Durant and the infant Union Pacific it certainly was. The large amount of newspaper coverage generated by the excursion alone would have made the venture worthwhile. But of more immediate importance, new money began to flow into the treasury of the company.

Not all of Durant's publicity schemes were merely flamboyant. He knew the Union Pacific was making history, a history that had to be recorded for the needs of posterity and the promotional enrichment of the railroad. To this end, he saw to it that a photographic record of construction was accumulated. In early 1868, Andrew J. Russell, official photographer to the construction corps of the United States Military Railroads during the Civil War, was employed by U.P. to help publicize the undertaking. By the time Russell reached the construction scene, the rails had progressed beyond Cheyenne, but he was still able to photograph construction progress for more than six hundred miles from Cheyenne to Promontory, Utah; moreover, during the next two years or more he combed the entire line from Omaha to Promontory, recording as no one else the construction and scenic wonders along the road for the curious East. His "views" were reproduced on stereoptican cards and sold in several series, gaining considerable popularity.

The quality of Russell's work is remarkable—a fact that stems from two sources. First, Russell was a supreme technician. For negative quality and reproduction of detail, his photographs were unsurpassed by any photographer of his day. He worked with a large format. Most of the photographs reproduced in this book are from contact prints from his original 10×13-inch glass-plate negatives. Second, Russell's original glass-plate negatives have been preserved and exist today, while the work of many other early-day photographers is known only from second- or third-generation copies of prints. The credit for the preservation of Russell's glass negatives must go to the American Geographical Society of New York, which carefully kept them preserved for more than twenty-eight years, many in their original crates. This generation owes much to that organization and to Thomas C. Durant's publicity-inspired impulse to document what most of the world considered "the great work of the age."

By the end of 1867, the Union Pacific's crews were wintering in Cheyenne, named by Dodge. By then, the original federal legislation that had limited the Central Pacific to building only to the Nevada line had been amended; now, both railroads were to build until they met. In the spring of 1868, Dodge pulled out all the stops, and by the end of the year the wild Irish track crews had spiked down the unbelievable total of four hundred twenty-five more miles and had reached the Utah border. During the early months of 1869, the Union Pacific completed enough track to bring them to Promontory Summit, Utah Territory, and the ceremony which symbolized the completion of the first transcontinental railroad: the driving of the Golden Spike on May 10, 1869.

The building of the Union Pacific Railroad was a project which caught the national fancy as, perhaps, no other in history. It was an undertaking so vast for the time that few people thought it could be accomplished at all. Civil War hero William Tecumseh Sherman, while a strong supporter of the project, privately admitted that "I would hate to buy a ticket on it for my grandchildren."

The rails were piercing a region unknown to most Americans, driving back the red man, bringing civilization in their wake, and uniting the nation. For a country so recently torn by rebellion, it provided a single great unifying project in which all could take pride.

For the men in the field charged with the responsibility of finding a path and laying down the iron, it was a monumental task filled with seemingly impossible difficulties and danger. Many died in the doing. And there was a larger significance, for these men were breaking down the last frontier, writing the first chapter of a work that could have only one end—the final settlement and form of the United States as one undivided nation.

Thomas C. Durant surveys a section of grading stretching west to infinity. The wooden bar resting on the ties is a track gauge used to measure and align distances between the rails.

Plate one, engine three. . . . In the yard at Omaha
A. J. Russell stopped a pony engine and its crew for
the first of his perfect images of the Work of the
Age. Nobody held entirely still for the long exposure, but the smell of iron and the gleam of brass,
the grip of the machine and the movement of a
man got through a glass window into history.

As photographer for Union Pacific Russell per-
sonally exposed more than two hundred 10 × 13-
inch, wet-plate, collodion negatives, and some four
hundred stereographic views of the road. In 1868,
when Russell went out into the wilds of Nebraska
and Wyoming, making a photograph was still a difficult and very specialized task, involving
preparation, exposure, and development of the
glass negative in immediate sequence, and the
transport of large and fragile sheets of glass (the
same size as the photograph opposite) in a jounc-
ing, horse-drawn darkroom. This was in itself a
feat to arouse the wonder and admiration of today's professional, with his handy Hasselblad,
equipped with interchangeable lenses and light
film magazines.

Omaha. . . . This was the supply base, the headquarters for the army of tracklayers thrown out west for a thousand miles. It was not until 1867 that any eastern road pushed as far west as the Missouri. Until then all supplies had to come up the river by steamboat or cross-country by wagon. Even in 1868, the river was still a break in the iron thread to the East, as no permanent bridge was put up for several years.

North Platte Bridge. . . . In the winter of 1866/67, the rails had reached, and gone a little beyond, the fork of the Platte River, where the north and south branches come together. This picture was taken at least two winters later. In the distance the flat Nebraska skyline is broken by new shops and a roundhouse solidly built of Wyoming stone. Two lines of telegraph cross the bridge on short poles jutting out from the framework. One belongs to Union Pacific, the other to Western Union.

Omaha. . . . By 1869, the railroad had moved so far west that the business of settlement and the attraction of immigrants to public and railroad lands alike were worth the construction of special cars for low-cost transportation of buyers and settlers. Here, in the newly finished carshops, the earliest of the crude transcontinental coaches, later memorialized by Robert Louis Stevenson and other impecunious cross-country travelers, were delivered to the narrow steel ribbon that unwound across the new lands from the Missouri to the Sacramento.

Sherman. . . . At eight thousand two hundred forty-two feet, the raw frontier village of Sherman was the highest point on the Union Pacific. When this view was made, construction crews were hundreds of miles to the west, but Sherman still had an "end-of-track" atmosphere.

Construction train at Granite Canyon. . . . The tracklaying crews had finished and moved on to somewhere west of Laramie by the time Russell made this view. One hundred years after this picture was taken, transportation experts started calling the practice of loading vehicles on railroad flatcars "piggybacking" and proclaimed it a new concept.

On the switch stand projecting out of the embankment on the far right are two pairs of phantom boots, left by owners who apparently changed their minds about being in the picture after all. The switch stand itself is evidence of the rush of construction. Time was not taken to grade the embankment to full width, only enough rock being thrown in to hold ties and rails, before the graders hurried on.

Approach to Dale Creek Bridge. . . . It was only a few miles beyond Sherman that the construction crews met one of their most spectacular bridge-building challenges: the Dale Creek Bridge. Here the route snaked through rocky ridges of granite. Trains slowed to a crawl before they reached the chasm.

Dale Creek Bridge. . . . One of Grenville Dodge's engineers called it "a big bridge for a small brook that one could easily step over." It was just that. Ribbonlike Dale Creek had cut a wide valley directly in the path of the advancing railroad builders. To span it, they built this engineering spectacle five hundred fifty miles west of Omaha and civilization. Formed of timbers cut to specification in Michigan, it measured seven hundred feet long, towered one hundred twenty-six feet above the streambed, and was guyed with ropes and wires against Wyoming winds and the shock of rolling trains. On April 23, 1868, it was finished, and Jack Casement's track-layers pushed on across it, hurrying into the wilderness.

General Grant at Fort Sanders, Summer, 1868. . . . Bridge-building and tracklaying are not the only problems facing Union Pacific's chief engineer Grenville M. Dodge. The congenial group posing here for Russell have just come from a showdown between Dodge and Thomas C. Durant, vice-president and chief promoter of the Union Pacific.

Durant, primarily interested in quick profits, had been altering Dodge's surveyed routes to increase profits for his secretly controlled, contract-letting operations. Dodge had balked, and the feud brought this distinguished group together, headed by Ulysses S. Grant, recently nominated for the Presidency.

Durant, in a characteristic slouch, is resting on the fence behind the tall, top-hatted figure of General Harney. Grant, looking the soul of determination, is to the left of center, almost directly in front of the bird cage. Framed in the doorway is General William Tecumseh Sherman. Second and third from the left are U.P. director Sidney Dillon and General Philip H. Sheridan. On the far left, as far from Durant as he can get, is Dodge.

Laramie Hotel. . . . Only a few months old in the fall of 1868, the railroad camp at Laramie had two thousand residents, some of whom stopped and peered from windows or assumed nonchalant poses on the platform of the combination dining hall and hotel. Cheyenne, Sherman, and the Black Hills lay behind them as the construction crews moved down the western slope.

Dining room at Laramie. . . . White tablecloths freshly laundered, silverware polished, china spotless and in place—everything is in readiness for a trainload of western travelers. Dark gleaming woodwork, kerosene chandeliers and imitation marble columns dramatically illustrate the civilizing effects of the railroad's western progress. Stagecoach road ranches usually had dirt floors. Rolling dining cars were still in the future in 1868, and trains made thirty-minute meal stops three times a day.

Wyoming Station. . . . A small way stop on the Little Laramie River, fifteen miles west of the town of Laramie itself, even Wyoming Station could have its proud day. Sunflower-stacked "No. 23" had been shined until a man could part his hair by his reflection in the steam dome just ahead of the cab. Many engines in this country sported antlers on their headlights, but "No. 23" boasted a particularly splendid set.

Directors' meeting. . . .Thomas C. Durant's private car suited the temperament of the man. It was a showpiece, extravagant and lavish for its time, with gilt work, crystal chandeliers, inlaid woodwork and twin mirrors.

Seated around the table are four of the more powerful figures behind the Union Pacific. Durant is the second from the right. Flanking Durant are two directors of the railroad. On his left is John Duff, veteran eastern railroad builder. On his right is Sidney Dillon, stern and somber, a perfect picture of how the trusty nineteenth-century railroad builder should appear. Both he and Duff later served as presidents of Union Pacific. Next to Dillon is Silas Seymour, consulting engineer, hired by Durant to engineer profits for him from the construction contracts. Described by associates as sly and devious, Seymour seems to live up to this description in Russell's photograph.

Machine Shops at Laramie

Windmill, Laramie. . . . Water was in scant supply on the Wyoming plains, and a monumental windmill and water tank had been erected at Laramie as part of the large rail complex abuilding. In the background is the proud twenty-stall roundhouse, behind it, the new machine shop. Both were built of stone brought in from Rock Creek, fifty miles to the west.

Her crew had brought brass-bound and newly painted "No. 80" out for the picture taking. A 4–4–0 "American" type, she was typical of the road engines used during construction. Her tender is filled with wood. The coalfields of Wyoming lie many miles beyond.

At the Green River. . . . By winter of 1868 the Green River had been reached and spanned. Casement's tracklaying forces were pushing so hard on the advance troops of graders and bridge builders that only a temporary bridge had been built here—and then the iron was down and the trains were moving through, westward from Citadel Rock.

Now the masons could take their time and build a bridge of lasting quality on the left. In the background, a water tank is evidence that once again good water is plentiful.

Working west of Green River, Casement's men set a tracklaying record for Union Pacific. In one day they pushed the iron rails seven and three-quarters miles. This record would stand only until spring, when the Central Pacific broke it by laying more than ten miles in a single day.

Building the permanent bridge, Green River. . . . Russell here studied the work of the bridge builders in detail, looking down from a vantage point on the temporary trestle. The crude but effective crane grasps the rock with a device like an ice tong; below, stone finishers and masons wait to lay the grout and wrestle the stone into place. There is snow on the ground, but the work is hard and several coats have already been shed. Russell managed to get himself into this picture. His shadow shows in the crevice to the right of center.

Jack Casement's outfit. . . . Three diamond-stack wood-burners pushed the work train forward, the Irishmen laying down the rails to make a path. The train was self-contained and designed for the job to be done. A workman's contemporary description closely resembles the train in this photograph: "Commencing from the west end [far left]—a flat car with tools, a forge for blacksmithing, then three long Pennsylvania passenger coaches they call 'sow belly' with three tiers of bunks on each side for sleeping, next the lounge car used for dining and sitting, next four box cars (one for cooking, one for baking, two for storage of supplies)."

The "sow bellies," far off to the left were apparently well named since the diamond bracing on their sides does not seem to have prevented a noticeable sag. It is winter, but even so the sleeping cars have been modified by one of the trackworkers' favorite tricks—that of pitching tents on the roofs of cars in order to escape the stifling atmosphere of the triple-tiered bunk cars.

Bear River City. . . . They called it Bear River City. Newspaper reporters from the East said it was the wildest end-of-track—"Hell on wheels"—town yet. Describing an earlier new town, one journalist commented on the contrast between the peaceful scene during the daytime and what happened once the sun went down: "At night, new aspects are presented in this city of premature growth. Watchfires gleam over the sea-like expanse of ground outside the city, while inside sol-diers, herdsmen, teamsters, women, railroad men are dancing, singing or gambling. I verily believe that there are men here who would murder a fellow creature for five dollars. Nay, there are men who have already done it, and who stalk abroad in daylight unwhipped of justice."

Leigh Freeman, who published the Frontier Index, a rolling end-of-track newspaper, was getting heartily sick of all this. He had

followed the railroad's progress more than seven hundred miles. Now, in Bear River City, he lashed out editorially against the gambling interests. On November 19, 1868, Freeman's enemies formed a mob, attacked the town, burned the jail and sacked the newspaper office. The railroad pushed on, and within a few months Bear River City was gone.

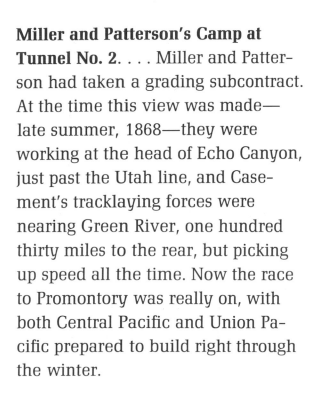

Miller and Patterson's Camp at Tunnel No. 2. . . . Miller and Patterson had taken a grading subcontract. At the time this view was made— late summer, 1868—they were working at the head of Echo Canyon, just past the Utah line, and Casement's tracklaying forces were nearing Green River, one hundred thirty miles to the rear, but picking up speed all the time. Now the race to Promontory was really on, with both Central Pacific and Union Pacific prepared to build right through the winter.

Jack Casement's outfit. . . . Russell took this picture to capture the star of the track forces, General John S. Casement, wearing a Cossack cap and fur-trimmed coat and carrying a bullwhip. The precision of Casement's Irish tracklayers mightily impressed newspaper correspondents from the East. Wrote one: "A light car, drawn by a single horse, gallops up to the front with its load of rails. Two men seize the end of a rail and start forward, the rest of the gang taking hold by twos, until it is clear of the car. They come forward at a run. At the word of command the rail is dropped in its place, right side up with care, while the same process goes on at the other side of the car. Less than thirty seconds to a rail for each gang, and so four rails go down to the minute. . . . Close behind the first gang come the gaugers, spikers, and bolters, and a lively time they make of it. It is a grand 'anvil chorus' . . . It is played in triple time, three strokes to the spike. There are 10 spikes to a rail, 400 rails to a mile, 1,800 miles to San Francisco—21,000,000 times are those sledges to be swung; 21,000,000 times are they to come down with their sharp punctuation before the great work of modern America is complete."

Weber Canyon tunnel. . . . With the graders working their way down into the Great Salt Lake Basin—down through the rugged Wasatch Mountains by way of Echo and Weber canyons—three tunnels were being drilled at once in the fall and winter of 1868. It was no stopping at this point, with the Central Pacific racing to capture the Salt Lake Basin.

Shaping timbers. . . . This is a closer view of Miller and Patterson's work on the Echo Tunnel, a job which would not be done before winter and the arrival of the tracklayers. Casement then would have to throw a temporary line around the graders.

Excavating in Weber Canyon

. . . .In the fall of 1868 grading parties were strung out like beads on a necklace all the way down Echo and Weber Canyons to Ogden, attacking every hill and ravine that barred the way. The Narrows began about four miles west of Echo and nine hundred ninety-five miles west of Omaha. This was some of the most difficult grading on the road, an almost continuous job of cut and fill.

As the picture shows, successive shelves were hacked into the rock, then pickaxed and blasted down to grade. Rough, temporary tracks have been laid in the foreground to haul rubble away. On the higher levels two-wheeled mule carts and wheelbarrows do the job.

Steam shovel at Hanging Rock. . . . The stories have been told and retold many times of how the Union Pacific was built almost by hand, with shovel and pick, primitive black powder, and horse-drawn carts. If so, what is a "steam Paddy" doing in the midst of the wilderness, nine hundred eighty-two miles west of Omaha?

Russell must have made this picture after the initial job was done—probably in the summer of 1869. The rails were first laid past Hanging Rock sometime in early January, 1869, when the countryside was deep in snow. Now, it is obviously summertime. Vegetation is growing on the hillside; the men are in shirt sleeves.

"No. 143" is hauling ballast, broken rock to fill in around ties and to widen embankments. The job of bringing stretches of hastily laid track up to standard was to go on continuously, even after the meeting of the rails at Promontory.

Echo City. . . . This picture moves back in time to the fall of 1868 and down the track to Echo City at the head of Weber Canyon. Unlike most of the other towns along the route, Echo City had a history that preceded the railroad. It had been a sturdy Mormon farming community for many years. Stagecoaches had a regular stop here and a pony express station still stood—the stone building at the foot of Pulpit Rock.

A Mormon family. . . . At Kaysville, Utah, this extended family lines up for posterity. Mary and Samuel Ashton (she is standing behind him in the doorway) are surrounded by her mother, three sisters, and five nieces and nephews. The minuscule accommodation provided by their sod-roofed cabin is a cause for wonderment.

Dan Casement and Clerks at Echo City. . . . The Casement
brothers were a team, Jack being the field boss, driving the
tracklayers at the front, his brother Dan handling the paper-
work, making sure the men were paid and supplies ordered.
Here Dan stands in the doorway, strategically placing his
clerks on the ground a few inches below him. Both Case-
ments were physically small men—but the men who worked
for them would swear the Casement boys were seven feet tall
and tough as nails. The second and third clerks from the left
may be suspected of recent military service. Their pants
mark them as veterans of the blue and gray.

Musicale. . . . The rather somber group of music makers
shown here were identified by Russell only as the "Rocky
Mountain Glee Club," probably drawn from the ranks of the
line's engineers and surveyors.

Tunnel No. 3, Weber Canyon. . . . The men in "No. 120's" crew have assumed their proper places; the engineer leans out of his cab, others man brake wheels on the boxcar and flatcars. Russell asked one man to go back to the tunnel entrance to demonstrate its scale.

The temporary bridge at Devil's Gate. . . . This bridge was going to cause a lot of trouble. The track-laying crews spiked their iron to it in February, 1869. Now, a month later, bridge engineer Leonard Eicholtz's men were still hard at work. The canyon walls constricted the river here, and the Weber, swollen by melting snow, put a serious strain on the bents, or vertical supporting pilings. Extra timbers were bolted in place and guy ropes strung to both banks.

It was all to be in vain. On May 5, just a few days before the planned ceremony at Promontory, heavy rains swelled the already rushing waters and undermined several supports. Union Pacific officials destined for the ceremony were caught on the wrong side.

Testing the new bridge, Devil's Gate. . . . Here Russell captured a scene so rich in detail it borders on illusion. Harsh mountain sunlight has chiseled every rock and crevice in sharp relief.

Three locomotives, three tenders, and two cars, though subordinate to the overall scene, can be studied down to the last bolt. Almost unnoticed are the people. But when the viewer begins to look for them they seem to be everywhere: on the river-bank, on the bridge, on the engines, in the cars, even in the bridge supports. Counting them becomes almost a game; there are at least a hundred people in the picture.

The "retouched" effect of the flowing river is the result of the comparatively long exposure required by the collodian negative. Russell's notes are seen reversed at the top of the plate.

The race to Promontory was over, and Russell had come back to Devil's Gate to record the testing of the new, permanent bridge. This was the reason for the three locomotives: to put as much weight on the bridge as possible.

One thousand miles from Omaha. . . .
The excursion party spreads its pic-
nic beneath "1000 Mile Tree." Some
of the Union Pacific's first tourists
picked the spot recommended in
their guidebook: "This living
milestone of Nature's planting has
long marked this place; long before
the hardy Mormon passed down this
wild gorge; long before the great
transcontinental railroad was even
thought of. It stood a lonely sentinel,
when all around was desolation. . . .
How changed the scene! The
ceaseless bustle of an active, pro-
gressive age, and hum of labor, the
roar and rush of the passing locomotive, has usurped the old quiet,
and henceforward the Lone Tree will
be, not a guide to the gloomy past,
but an index of the coming greatness
of a regenerated country."

Telegraph corps at Weber Canyon
. . . . Russell was back at the front again in the spring of 1869. The tracklayers were not far ahead, for the rough log ties were still unballasted—even with the minimum of rock thrown between them during initial construction.

Keeping pace with the end-of-track, the telegraph workers maintained continuous, if tenuous, communication between the front line forces and headquarters in Omaha. When the last spike was driven the telegraph lines were there also, to broadcast the news to a waiting nation.

During the early years of the railroad the thin copper wire was one of the favorite targets of raiding Indians. Rails and ties proved a strenuous job to disrupt, but the wires were easy to strip down, and they made attractive bracelets and necklaces.

Temple Street, Salt Lake City. . . . Commerce was the theme of Temple Street, with retail stores of every variety lining both sides. Every variety, that is, except dealers in alcoholic beverages. On the far side several stores displayed the crest of Zion's Cooperative Mercantile Institution—or ZCMI. This cooperative venture was organized in 1868 by Mormon leaders to purchase goods in large quantities and to solve the problem of a lack of currency.

Salt Lake City had been bypassed to the north by the railroad—just as had Denver earlier. Dodge had wanted to find a line through Salt Lake City and around the south end of the lake but finally gave up. It would have added seventy-six miles, many steeper grades, and about $2,500,000 in cost to the already strained railroad. The unpleasant task of telling Brigham Young fell on Dodge's shoulders. The Mormon leader was furious. He threatened to throw all his support and labor supply to Central Pacific if they would choose a southern route. But C.P. agreed with Dodge, and Young finally consented to help both railroads and rely on a branch line to serve Salt Lake City.

Salt Lake City. . . . An oasis of settlement in the western wilderness, Salt Lake City had been growing for more than twenty years when the photographer Russell arrived. While the Saints looked with profound disapproval upon the rip-roaring antics of such railroad towns as Corinne, they were not averse to accepting their share of the railroad's largess. Brigham Young himself accepted a grading contract from U. P., and a bishop took on the C. P. contract. At left center of the picture is Brigham Young's house.

Corinne. . . . A city of an entirely different sort from the Mormon capital is here caught in Russell's lens. Corinne, north of Ogden, and just twenty-eight miles from Promontory Summit, did not lack for saloons or entertainment for the railroad workers. In March, 1869, a newspaper reporter described the new town as "built of canvas and board shanties. The place is fast becoming civilized, several men having been killed there already; the last one was found in the river with four bullets in him." He went on to venture that between Promontory Summit and Brigham City, thirty-six miles east, there were three hundred whiskey shops, all "developing the resources of the territory . . . There are many heavy contractors on the Promontory, but the heaviest firm I have heard of is named 'Red Jacket' [whiskey]. I notice nearly every wagon that passes have a great many boxes marked with his name."

In the final weeks of construction thousands of Irish track workers and Mormon graders swarmed over this countryside. However, their diets were not entirely liquid. Three of the nearest buildings in this photograph are eating houses. All offer the same price: "Meals 50¢." Even more interesting is a building at the far left: "Corinne Book Store."

At the paymaster's car, Promontory. . . . They ate beef and bread and washed it down with strong black coffee, though whiskey was their favorite drink. They bathed only when there was a stream nearby—and at Promontory the nearest water was four miles away.

When they started in Omaha they numbered only about two hundred fifty. At Promontory they were ten thousand strong. Only about one in four were tracklayers. The others were graders, teamsters, herdsmen, cooks, bakers, blacksmiths, bridge builders, carpenters, masons, and clerks. On the average they made three dollars a day, good wages for the times.

Many were Irish. Most had fought in the Civil War and still wore parts of their old uniforms. They had another thing in common: they were proud of a job nearly done—a staggering undertaking few serious people thought could be done in twice the time.

Supply Trains at a siding. . . . In April, 1869, both railroads were building furiously toward the meeting point. Congress had decided the rails should come together at Promontory Summit, a circular basin at the crest of the Promontory Mountains, which form a ridge jutting into the Great Salt Lake from the north. Central Pacific was climbing the west face; Union Pacific crews were blasting and spiking track on the steeper east face. Here, one of Casement's work trains is unloading supplies to be carried forward in freight wagons.

It had not been until April 10 that a joint resolution of Congress had finally set the precise meeting point. Until then it looked quite likely that both sides would continue building right on past each other, trying to capture as much territory as possible. Indeed, at least one hundred miles of duplicate, parallel grade had already been built. At times the competing graders worked within a hundred yards of each other, sometimes setting off their blasting charges with no warning to the other side.

Promontory Trestle. . . . Engine No. 119, with a full head of steam, is working her way up to the meeting with Central Pacific over the newly completed trestle. Now all the track work has been done. Only a small gap has been left for the ceremony.

They have called this span the "Big Trestle." It was the last serious obstacle on the east face of the Promontory. These last miles were hard, the grade rising eight hundred feet in just ten miles. The trestle was four hundred feet long, eighty-five feet high, and was built in thirty-eight days and nights. Its frailness caused comment in the press. One San Francisco correspondent did not try to hide his bias for his home-state railroad and predicted that Union Pacific's trestle "will shake the nerves of the stoutest hearts of railroad travellers when they see what a few feet of round timbers and seven-inch spikes are expected to uphold a train in motion."

Evidence of the two roads' parallel grading shows up in Russell's photograph. The unused Central Pacific grade lies just uphill from Union Pacific's. Both grades cut through a rocky spine on the far side of the ravine. Another parallel cut can be seen directly above the first flatcar.

Promontory town. . . . Although Russell took this picture in October, 1869, the character of Promontory had not changed. An observer characterized it later as being "4,900 feet above sea level, though, theologically speaking, if we interpret scripture literally, it ought to have been 49,000 feet below that level; for it certainly was, for its size, morally nearest to the infernal regions of any town on the road."

Promontory was even more transient than Corinne. Within ten years the board-and-canvas town was almost deserted; by 1903 a shortcut across the lake bypassed the historic spot, and in 1942 the last rails remaining were pulled up and donated to the war effort.

Assembling to lay the last rail. . . .
At Promontory, Union Pacific rails
approached from the north. In this
photograph they appear in the foreground, the camera looking south
and a little west. A space has been
left for the laying of the last rails;
behind the crowd are several Central Pacific cars and at least one
locomotive.

Chinese laying the last rail. . . . Union Pacific's Irishmen laid the next to last rail. Central Pacific's Chinese workmen laid the final rail—in the foreground—and drove a few spikes at one end to hold it in place. This rail was to be the focal point of the ceremony.

Probably the man with his back to the camera in the foreground and the man with boots planted firmly on either side of a tie in the center are Chinese. But the taller Irishmen, mugging for the photographer, dominate the picture. It is said that someone shouted to one of the photograhers, "Take a shot!" The Chinese, who knew only one definition for the word "shot," dropped their rail and dove for the dirt.

Engineers of the Union Pacific. . . . By 10:30 A.M., May 10, 1869, Union Pacific's official train had arrived carrying officers of the railroad, including Grenville M. Dodge and Thomas C. Durant. Dodge appears here seventh from the right. Durant, the ranking U.P. official at the ceremony, was in his car, nursing a severe headache.

Durant's headache may well have been born two days earlier while he was being held prisoner by his own workmen at Piedmont, Wyoming Territory. They had surrounded Durant's car—blocked by floodwaters in Weber Canyon—and refused to let him move until they received five months' back pay. Durant hastily wired for $500,000 and paid off the men. But the kidnapping, coupled with the rain-damaged track, delayed the festivities at Promontory two days beyond the original schedule. From Saturday, May 8, they were held over until Monday.

The ceremony starts. . . . By happy chance three companies of the 21st U.S. Infantry had arrived. They were on their way from Omaha to the Presidio at San Francisco. The regimental band was with them, and its brave strains brightened the gathering. It was 12 noon. Little flags fluttered on the "Jupiter," Central Pacific's engine, in the foreground. The camera is facing north and "Jupiter's" large funnel-shaped smokestack dominates the foreground. Union Pacific's "No. 119" uses a standard straight stack. The broad stack was common to wood-burning locomotives working in forested territories. A wire screen was stretched across the top to stop sparks and prevent fires along the right-of-way.

Officers of Union Pacific. . . . It is now just about noon and the ceremonies are to begin at any minute. Durant has made it out into the crowd, although it looks as though his headache is not getting any better. He is (1), identified in the inset at right. Russell has asked all to take off their hats so their faces won't be in shadow. The sunlight hurts Durant's eyes.

Details of the ceremony had been in doubt until just a few minutes before the show. Officials of the two roads could not agree who was to deliver which blows to the last spikes. California had provided the ceremonial gold spikes and Central Pacific had begun construction first. Union Pacific had built the longest distance, and was certainly foremost in the minds of the nation. At one point the argument had grown so warm Union Pacific officials threatened to boycott the ceremony and not join the rails at all.

Making up the front row are: (1) Thomas C. Durant, Vice-President; (2) Rev. Dr. John Todd, who was to deliver the benediction; (3) Miss Minerva Earll, sister of (4) Mrs. Samuel Reed; (5) her daughter, Anna Reed; (6) John Duff, Director; (7) Sidney Dillon, Director; (8) Silas Seymour, Consulting Engineer; (9) Grenville M. Dodge, Chief Engineer; (10) Samuel Reed, Superintendent of Construction.

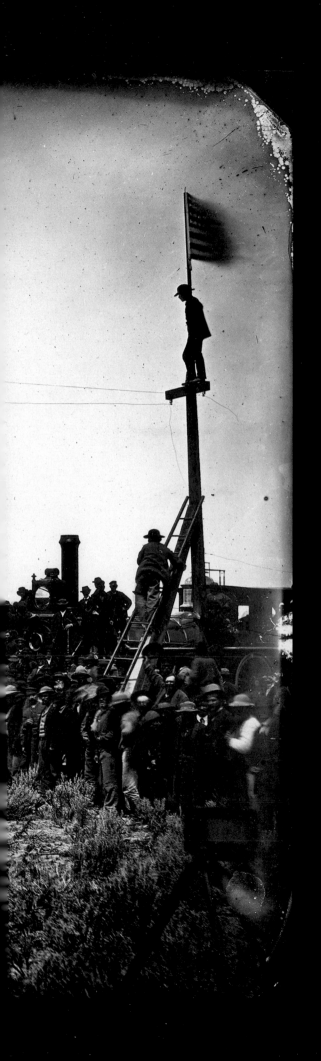

Omaha Telegraph:

TO EVERYBODY: KEEP QUIET. WHEN THE LAST SPIKE IS DRIVEN . . . WE WILL SAY "DONE." DON'T BREAK THE CIRCUIT, BUT WATCH FOR THE BLOWS OF THE HAMMER.

Promontory Telegraph:

ALMOST READY. HATS OFF. PRAYER IS BEING OFFERED.

Chicago Telegraph:

WE UNDERSTAND. ALL ARE READY IN THE EAST.

Promontory Telegraph:

ALL READY NOW. THE SPIKE WILL SOON BE DRIVEN. THE SIGNAL WILL BE THREE DOTS FOR THE COMMENCEMENT OF THE BLOWS.

W. N. Shilling handled the telegraph, working from the small table at trackside. He had a nationwide hookup, the first in history. The crowd kept pushing in and blocking his view and that of the photographers. Finally, amid loud cheers the laurel tie was slipped into place. The golden spike was inserted into a specially drilled hole; no one struck it. The **last** spike was polished iron! Telegrapher Shilling had set wires in advance so that the blows to the iron would signal the rest of the nation. Stanford and Durant did the honors.

Promontory Telegraph:

DOT. DOT. DOT. DONE.

East and West Shaking Hands. . . . Done! A double band of iron stretched from Omaha to San Francisco. East and West were met and permanently forged together, the Work of an Age completed, Manifest Destiny achieved.

Despite all the flowery and momentous pronouncements that preceded, now general hilarity broke loose. Whistle shrieking, "No. 119" moved forward, prodding spectators aside. She crossed the spike and moved up to the "Jupiter." Grenville M. Dodge and Central Pacific Chief Engineer Samuel S. Montague shook hands.